shiny gods
finding freedom from things that distract us

Leader Guide

Program Components

Book
shiny gods: finding freedom from things that distract us

DVD
shiny gods: finding freedom from things that distract us
Video programs with downloadable leader guide

Program Flash Drive with Booklet
first: putting GOD first in living and giving
Instructions for planning and using the program

Devotions
first: putting GOD first in living and giving
Daily meditations to use during the program

Youth Study Edition
first: putting GOD first in living and giving
Book for youth to use during the program, with leader helps

Children's Leader Guide
first: putting GOD first in living and giving
Lesson plans for younger and older children

Program Kit
first: putting GOD first in living and giving
One of each component

Mike Slaughter

shiny gods

finding freedom from things that distract us

Leader Guide

by Ella Robinson

Abingdon Press

Nashville

Mike Slaughter

shiny gods
finding freedom from things that distract us

Leader Guide
by Ella Robinson

ISBN 978-1-4267-6196-6

Library of Congress Cataloging-in-Publication applied for.

13 14 15 16 17 18 19 20 21 22—10 9 8 7 6 5 4 3 2 1

Contents

Introduction

A study done in spring 2012 indicates that two-thirds of Americans are living paycheck to paycheck.[1] People are consumed with debt and the fear of going deeper into debt. However, the cause may not be our lack of money, but instead our penchant for viewing luxuries as essential items. We expect to have cable television, mobile phones, and the latest computer games. As we turn these luxuries into essentials, we allow them to become what pastor and author Mike Slaughter calls "shiny gods."

In his book and DVD, *shiny gods: finding freedom from things that distract us*, Slaughter helps us identify our own shiny distractions and then encourages us to put God first in all aspects of life. We are inspired to release our resources—time, money, and talents—fully into God's hands. The book and DVD are suitable for individual use or, with the help of this leader guide, can be used in a small group study for adults.

This book, DVD, and leader guide can be used as part of a four-week churchwide stewardship program titled *first: putting GOD first in living and giving*, which also includes a program guide on flash drive, a book of devotions, and parallel studies for youth and children.

For the *shiny gods* small group study, participants will read one chapter of the book prior to the study session, then will meet together for group study each week for four weeks. During the group study, participants will view a video from the accompanying DVD that will provide additional information for the week's study.

For groups that want to spend an additional week studying the book's conclusion, "What's Next?," we have included a fifth week's session plan in the adult, youth, and children's studies.

For the adult small group study, provide each participant with a copy of the *shiny gods* book enough in advance of the first study session so that they can read the introduction and first chapter and be prepared for group discussion. You may want to have extra copies of the book available at the first meeting in case people who join the group at that meeting can take a copy of the book home and use it to prepare for the next week's session.

Encourage group members to underline or highlight portions of each chapter as they read. Suggest that they obtain a spiral-bound notebook or journal for this study to note questions or essential points that they would like to make during the group sessions.

Assure participants who may have already read *shiny gods* that their participation in the study will enhance their understanding of the book. Although the material in the book will be familiar to them, watching the videos and participating in group discussions will give them a new learning experience and an opportunity for spiritual growth. Ask participants who have read the book before to read it again, one chapter per week, along with the other group members. Not only will this refresh their memory, but it will also provide them with new insight and understanding.

The DVD for this study contains one video for each session. As the group leader, you should preview each segment of the DVD before showing it to your group. If one or more group members miss a meeting, arrange for them to see the video outside the regular meeting time. Also, give them a copy of the week's participant handout that is included at the end of each chapter in this Leader Guide.

How to Use This Leader Guide

As group leader, your role will be to facilitate the weekly sessions using this Leader Guide and the accompanying DVD. Because no two groups are alike, this guide has been designed to give you flexibility and choice in tailoring the sessions for your group. You may choose one of the following format options, *or adapt these as you wish to meet the schedule and needs of your particular group.* (Note: The times indicated within parentheses are merely estimates. You may move at a faster or slower pace, making adjustments as necessary to fit your schedule.)

Basic Option: 60 minutes

Opening Prayer	(2 minutes)
Biblical Foundation	(3 minutes)
Video Presentation	(15 minutes)
Group Discussion	(30 minutes)
Taking It Home	(5 minutes)
Closing Prayer	(less than 5 minutes)

Extended Option: 90 minutes

Opening Prayer	(2 minutes)
Biblical Foundation	(3 minutes)
Opening Activity	(10–15 minutes)
Video Presentation	(15 minutes)
Group Discussion	(30 minutes)
Group Activity	(15 minutes)
Taking It Home	(5 minutes)
Closing Prayer	(less than 5 minutes)

Although you are encouraged to adapt the sessions to meet your needs, you also are encouraged to make prayer and Scripture reading regular components of the weekly group sessions. Feel free to use the opening and closing prayers provided here, or to create your own prayers. In either case, the intent is to "cover" the group session in prayer, acknowledging that only because of God's mercy and grace have our sins been forgiven. Scripture verses provided for each session are intended to serve as a biblical foundation for the group session, as well as for participants' continuing reflection during the following week.

In addition to the session components listed above, the following leader helps are provided to equip you for each group session:

Fundamentals: materials to gather for the meeting
Key Insights: summary of main points from the week's content
Leader Background: additional information related to topic
Notable Quote: noteworthy quote relating to the week's content

You may use these helps for your personal preparation only, or you may choose to incorporate them into the group session in some way. For example, you might choose to review the key insights from the video either before or after group discussion, incorporate the leader extra into group discussion, or close with the Notable Quote.

At the end of the materials provided for each group session, you will find a reproducible participant handout. This handout includes key insights and Taking It Home application exercises for the coming week. Each week, you will have the opportunity to remind participants that these exercises are designed to help them get the most out of this study that they possibly can. They alone are the ones who will determine whether or not this is just another group study or a transformational experience that will have a lasting, positive impact on their lives.

Helpful Hints

Here are a few hints for preparing and leading the weekly group sessions.

- Become familiar with the material before the group session. If possible, watch the DVD segment in advance.
- Choose the various components you will use during the group session, including the specific discussion questions you plan to cover. (Highlight these or put a checkmark beside them.) Remember, you do not have to use all the questions provided, and you can create your own.
- Secure a TV and DVD player in advance; oversee room setup.
- Begin and end on time.
- Be enthusiastic. Remember, you set the tone for the class.
- Create a climate of participation, encouraging individuals to participate as they feel comfortable.

- Communicate the importance of group discussions and group exercises.
- To stimulate group discussion, consider reviewing the key insights first and then asking participants to tell what they saw as the highlights of the video.
- If no one answers at first, don't be afraid of a little silence. Count to seven silently; then say something such as, "Would anyone like to go first?" If no one responds, venture an answer yourself. Then ask for comments and other responses.
- Model openness as you share with the group. Group members will follow your example. If you share at a surface level, everyone else will follow suit.
- Draw out participants without asking them to share what they are unwilling to share. Make eye contact with someone and say something such as, "How about someone else?"
- Encourage multiple answers or responses before moving on.
- Ask "Why?" or "Why do you believe that?" to help continue a discussion and give it greater depth.
- Affirm others' responses with comments such as, "Great" or "Thanks" or "Good insight"—especially if this is the first time someone has spoken during the group session.
- Give everyone a chance to talk, but keep the conversation moving. Moderate to prevent a few individuals from doing all of the talking.
- Monitor your own contributions. If you are doing most of the talking, back off so that you do not train the group not to respond.
- Remember that you do not have to have all the answers. Your job is to keep the discussion going and encourage participation.

- Honor the time schedule. If a session is running longer than expected, get consensus from the group before continuing beyond the agreed upon ending time.
- Consider involving group members in various aspects of the group session, such as asking for volunteers to run the DVD, to read the prayers or say their own, to read the Scripture, and so forth.

Above all, remember to pray. Pray for God to prepare and guide you; pray for your group members by name and for whatever God may do in their hearts and lives, and pray for God's presence and leading before each group session. Prayer will both encourage and empower you for the weeks ahead.

Finally, if you are a first-time leader, remember that many characters in the Bible were hesitant and unsure of accepting God's call to lead, but God imparted the ability in each of them to step out in faith and obedience. Rest assured that God will be with you as you follow. Claim Paul's words: "I can do all this through him who gives me strength" (Philippians 4:13 TNIV).

1. Naming Our Idols

Planning the Session

Fundamentals

1. Confirm your meeting place and time.
2. Secure a TV and DVD player and ensure that they are operational.
3. Obtain extra copies of the *shiny gods* book to have on hand so that each participant will have a copy to use during the study session.
4. Have extra Bibles available for participants to use during the study session.
5. Secure paper and pencils for participants to use during a group activity.
6. If your meeting area has Internet access, secure one or more computers and the necessary information for connecting to the Internet.

Session Goals

This session is intended to help participants...

* identify their own personal "shiny gods"—the modern-day cultural idols that distract us.

- realize that even gifts from God can become idols when they are assigned a wrong priority.
- understand that virtues can become vices when not directed toward Jesus.
- define a covenant relationship with God.
- realize that worshiping cultural idols will negatively affect children.

Key Insights

1. Idolatry is not a new problem for the human race. Cultural groups throughout history—the Canaanites, the Aztecs, and, yes, modern-day Americans—have placed objects before God.
2. Idols are not always sculptures or graven images. Author Mike Slaughter defines an idol as anything, or anyone that receives the primary focus of our energy or resources, which should first belong to God.
3. God's beautiful gifts to us can become idols when we assign to them a wrong priority. Even our virtues can become vices—or idols—if they are not directed toward Jesus.
4. Shiny gods distract us from experiencing God's generosity.
5. The Bible uses the word *covenant* regarding a bond between people in which each party places the other person's priorities above his or her own. Clearly the word applies to our relationship with God, too.
6. Idolatry will negatively affect children. Ordinarily, children and grandchildren will not adopt a person's stated beliefs; they will adopt the person's passions.
7. In our idolatry, we have imagined ourselves to be the center of our universe. We view all of our interests by how well they serve us.

Leader Background

- The word *jealous* used in the Old Testament is related to the word *zealous*. A person who is jealous and one being zealous are experiencing similar emotions. The Bible refers to God as being zealous in protecting that which is precious to him.
- Human jealousy is selfish and sinful. We often try to hurt others. For example, Joseph's brothers were jealous of him and wanted to harm him.
- In ancient times, a *covenant* was a ceremonious event that sealed a legally binding action. It was much more than a contract that we think of today. Two of the most familiar biblical covenants are God's covenant with Noah (Genesis 9) and God's covenant with Abraham (Genesis 15). God's covenant with man is unique in that we enter into an obligation with God, but God takes on the consequences if the covenant is not fulfilled.

Getting Started

Opening Prayer

Heavenly God, as we begin this study, help us to recognize the earthly temptations and distractions that are making us ineffective in serving you. Open our eyes so that we will see you clearly; open our ears so that we will hear your voice, and open our hearts so that we will become a vessel for your use. We praise your name, Lord, and lift our thanksgiving to you for your unending grace and mercy. Bless us as we seek your will. Amen.

Biblical Foundation

The idols of the nations are silver and gold, made by human hands. They have mouths, but cannot speak, eyes, but cannot see. They have ears, but cannot hear, nor is there breath in their mouths. (Psalm 135:15-17 TNIV)

Opening Activity

Explain to the group about the study done in spring 2012 (described in the Introduction both in this Leader Guide and Slaughter's book *shiny gods*) that indicated two-thirds of Americans are living paycheck to paycheck. Point out that the cause of this situation may not be our lack of money, but instead our penchant for viewing luxuries as essential expenses.

Lead the group in a general discussion of this concept as it relates to their lifestyles. When everyone has had a chance to share their thoughts, hand out paper and pencils and ask each participant to take a few quiet moments to list his or her own shiny gods. Tell them that they will not discuss their lists as a group, but that they should keep the list to refer to throughout this study.

Learning Together

Video Presentation

Play Session 1: "Naming Our Idols"
Running Time: 10:33

Group Discussion

When we think about idolatry, we usually think about graven images—golden calves, silver statues—that were worshiped during biblical times. Or we might think of religions other than Christianity. So why are we, twentieth-century Christians, focusing on idolatry?

An idol is anything, or anyone, that receives the primary focus of our energy or resources, which should first belong to God. One of the earliest accounts of idolatry is in the Book of Exodus. While Moses was on Mount Sinai receiving the Ten Commandments, his brother Aaron took gold jewelry from the people and turned it into the image of a calf, and the people immediately declared the lump of gold to be a god.

Lead the group in a discussion of other examples of idol worship in the Old and New Testaments. Then ask them to think of and discuss idols in their own lives.

The Bible refers to separating the primary focus of our energies and resources from God as having a "divided heart." Today, as in biblical times, Christians place their focus on earthly things instead of on God. When we separate our spiritual life from the practical elements of life, we use our possessions, our values, and our traditions as idols to provide identity or meaning in our lives. We are worshipping God's gifts instead of God, the Giver.

In the book and video, Mike Slaughter discusses football as an idol in modern America. Lead participants in a discussion of football, sports, and other cultural phenomena as modern-day idols.

One use of the word *covenant* in the Bible is to describe the marriage relationship, in which a bond exists in which both parties are to serve the other person's priorities above their own. When we are in a covenant relationship with God, we give God our full-time, everyday worship. Lead participants in a discussion of covenant relationships with people and with God, then invite them to try the group activity below.

Group Activity (choose one)

- Give each participant a piece of white or light-colored construction paper and pieces of brightly colored chalk or artist pastels. Ask them to use their chalk to write *2 Kings 17:41* on the construction paper. When everyone has finished writing, read the verse to the group. Explain that as the chalk has rubbed off on your fingers, your passions rub off on your children. If we worship shiny gods, our children will worship them also.
- If your meeting place has Internet access, view the YouTube video at http://www.youtube.com/

watch?v=QPil9Br-5lE.[2] Lead a discussion of the nation's infatuation with sports. Point out that sports is a good thing, but it should not be valued above God.

Wrapping Up

Taking It Home

Explain that there are two resources available to help participants with personal application each week. First, there is the participant handout. Briefly review the Taking It Home application exercises included on the handout. Encourage participants to complete the activities during the coming week.

Second, there is the *shiny gods* book, which expands on the material covered in the weekly video presentations. Suggest that participants read the second chapter this week to prepare for the next group session. If participants have not ordered or purchased copies of the book yet, encourage them to do so now.

Notable Quote

If we are full of pride and conceit, and ambition and self-seeking, and pleasure and the world, there is no room for the Spirit of God; and I believe many a man is praying to God to fill him when he is full already with something else.[3]

—Dwight L. Moody

Closing Prayer

Lord God, we are grateful for your word and the opportunity to learn about the mercy and grace that you so generously give to us. In this lesson we have discovered that almost all our idols are really good gifts from you, to which we have assigned a wrong priority. As we continue our study in the weeks ahead, help us to align our priorities so that we can focus on you and your mission for the world. Amen.

1. Naming Our Idols Participant Handout

"Do not forget the covenant I have made with you, and do not worship other gods. Rather, worship the LORD your God; it is he who will deliver you from the hand of all your enemies."
(2 Kings 17:38-39 TNIV)

Key Insights
1. Idolatry is not a new problem for the human race. Cultural groups throughout history—the Canaanites, the Aztecs, and, yes, modern-day Americans—have placed objects before God.
2. Idols are not always sculptures or graven images. Author Mike Slaughter defines an idol as anything, or anyone that receives the primary focus of our energy or resources, which should first belong to God.
3. God's beautiful gifts to us can become idols when we assign to them a wrong priority. Even our virtues can become vices—or idols—if they are not directed toward Jesus.
4. Shiny gods distract us from experiencing the generosity of God.
5. The Bible uses the word *covenant* regarding a bond between people in which each party places the other person's priorities above his or her own. Clearly the word applies to our relationship with God, too.
6. Idolatry will negatively affect children. Ordinarily, children and grandchildren will not adopt a person's stated beliefs; they will adopt the person's passions.
7. In our idolatry, we have imagined ourselves to be the center of our universe. We view all of our interests by how well they serve us.

Taking It Home

- Make a list of the ways that you spent your time yesterday.
- Make another list of the ways you spent your money yesterday.
- Look at the two lists. What do they tell you about your priorities?
- What actions do you need to take in order to adjust your priorities, and why?

2. Money, Work, and Debt

Planning the Session

Fundamentals

1. Confirm your meeting place and time.
2. Secure a TV and DVD player and ensure that they are operational.
3. Obtain extra copies of the book *shiny gods* to have on hand so that each participant will have a copy to use during the study session.
4. Have extra Bibles available for participants to use during the study session.
5. Secure paper and pencils for participants to use during a group activity.
6. For the Opening Activity below, collect a variety of bags with store names on them, some from grocery stores, department stores, drugstores, home improvement stores, dress shops, shoe stores, and so forth. Place an item in each bag that is unrelated to the bag type—for example, an inexpensive but pretty piece of jewelry in a grocery bag, or a tube of toothpaste in a dress shop bag.

7. Make a handout of credit statistics found at Internet web-sites such as http://www.creditcards.com/credit-card-news/credit-card-industry-facts-personal-debt-statistics-1276.php[4] and www.consolidatedcredit.org/credit-card-debt/consumer-debt-facts/#back.[5] You may want to include some of the credit card information found in the Leader Extra below. Make enough copies for each participant to have one.

8. Obtain magazines and newspapers that can be cut, along with scissors, glue sticks, tape, construction paper, and markers.

Session Goals

This session is intended to help participants...

- understand that we put ourselves into the bondage of debt when we view luxuries as essentials.
- realize that no matter how much debt we have, there is always hope.
- understand the two kinds of debt—consumer debt and investment debt.
- understand that work is a gift from God for us to use in serving him and his kingdom.

Key Insights

1. The drive to fulfill our idea of obtaining "enough" keeps us indebted and always seeking the next source of satisfaction. God offers us freedom from this obsession.
2. Debt is one of the greatest bondages in America today.
3. Work is a gift from God. We work to serve God's creation.
4. The primary objective of work is *outcome*, not income.
5. The way we work teaches children what it means to accept personal responsibility.
6. No matter what our debt situation is, there is always hope.
7. Using a credit card to accumulate ongoing debt is not acting within God's means of provision.

8. There are two kinds of debt—consumer debt and investment debt.
9. We need to develop a strategic plan to get out of debt as soon as possible.
10. Financial freedom is the result of a lifestyle obedient to the word of God.
11. It's always better to live smaller and more simply than to go into debt.

Leader Background

- A large portion of debt nationwide is due to carrying a balance on credit cards. As the credit card balance increases, so does the financial hardship for many Americans.
- By the end of 2008, 176.8 million Americans held credit cards. On average, each one of those held 3.5 credit cards, and this number increases each year. This means there are more than 600 million credit cards being used in America.
- As of December 2011, the total U.S. consumer debt (including credit card debt) reached $2.5 trillion.
- On average, today's consumer has a total of 13 credit obligations on record at a credit bureau.
- Twenty-six percent of Americans admit to not paying their bills on time.[6]
- In 2010, Americans spent over $15 billion on video games and video game content alone, according to TechSpot: Technology News and Analysis.[7]
- According to "Ten Things Americans Waste the Most Money On," the "average American household," which has an income of $63,000, spends more than $8,000 on goods and services it does not actually need.[8]

Getting Started

Opening Prayer

Gracious Heavenly God, we praise your name. Draw us nearer to you, Lord, as we study your word. Quiet the earthly clamor that fills our minds, and teach us to turn our attention to you. Amen.

Biblical Foundation

"What good will it be for you to gain the whole world, yet forfeit your soul?" (Matthew 16:26 TNIV)

Opening Activity

Using the shopping bags and items obtained prior to the meeting (see above), make an attractive display of the bags on a table so that participants can see them as they come in the door. Ask each participant to select a bag, then lead participants to discuss why they selected the bag. Were they attracted by a name brand? Did they like the bag's color or design? Did they want what the bag represents? What about the item in the bag? Was the gift deceptive?

Learning Together

Video Presentation

Play Session 2: Money, Work, and Debt
Running Time: 10:20

Group Discussion

One of the greatest bondages in America today, in many of our lives, is the bondage of debt. It is not God's intention for us to be buried under the burdens of financial worry. However, we must apply God's directives for financial freedom, which means not worshipping the "shiny gods" of consumerism and giving our energy and focus to them. We also need to understand why we work.

Author Mike Slaughter says, "We don't primarily work for the income; we work for the outcome. We work for the significance we find through serving God's creation." Lead participants to discuss the work they do. Point out that some participants may have full-time jobs outside the home, others may be homemakers, and others may be college students, but all of us have work to do. Work is something bigger than simply earning sustenance.

When we recognize that work is God's means of providing for us, we can understand the nature of debt. Ask participants to turn to Chapter 2 of the book *shiny gods* and note the two negative approaches to work: the danger of minimizing work; and the opposite danger of placing the work above the source, which is God. Point out another that negative approach is compromising our integrity in our work. Ask a participant to read aloud Proverbs 11:1 and Proverbs 22:1. Then lead a discussion of how our attitude and approach to work is a reflection of our commitment to God.

If you prepared handouts ahead of time on credit card debt, distribute them now.

Explain that there are two kinds of debt: consumer debt and investment debt. Ask participants to explain the difference between these two kinds of debt, then lead in the group activity described below.

Group Activity

Ask participants to form two groups. Provide each group with a table to work on; several magazines and newspapers that can be cut; and scissors, glue sticks, tape, construction paper, and markers.

Explain that there are two kinds of debt: consumer debt and investment debt. Ask one group to search the magazines and newspapers on their table for examples of consumer debt, then cut out pictures and words to create a collage of their findings. Ask the other group to do the same for investment debt. When both groups have finished their collages, ask them to show their collages to the larger group and explain what they found. Continue the discussion of consumer debt and investment debt.

Wrapping Up

Taking It Home

Explain that there are two resources available to help participants each week. First, there is the Participant Handout. Briefly review the Taking It Home application exercises included on the handout. Encourage participants to complete the activities during the coming week.

Second, there is Mike Slaughter's accompanying book, *shiny gods*, which expands on the material covered in the weekly video presentations. Suggest that participants read the third chapter this week in preparation for next week's group session. There still may be participants who have not ordered or purchased copies of the book. If so, encourage them to do so now.

Notable Quote

"The more we invest in God's kingdom, his service, his time through our tithing and giving, the more he invests in us."[9]

—Sara

Closing Prayer

Heavenly God, forgive us for allowing the lure of greater wealth and the accumulation of things to occupy our lives.

Help us to change our focus, to see how we can use the wealth and things that you have so graciously given us to your service. Shower us with your mercy and shield us from temptation. Amen.

2. Money, Work, and Debt Participant Handout

The Lord will open the heavens, the storehouse of his bounty, to send rain on your land in season and to bless all the work of your hands. (Deuteronomy 28:12 TNIV)

Key Insights
1. The drive to fulfill our idea of obtaining "enough" keeps us indebted and always seeking the next source of satisfaction. God offers us freedom from this obsession.
2. Debt is one of the greatest bondages in America today.
3. Work is a gift from God. We work to serve God's creation.
4. The primary objective of work is *outcome*, not income.
5. The way we work teaches children what it means to accept personal responsibility.
6. No matter what our debt situation is, there is always hope.
7. Using a credit card to accumulate ongoing debt is not acting within God's means of provision.
8. There are two kinds of debt—consumer debt and investment debt.
9. We need to develop a strategic plan to get out of debt as soon as possible.
10. Financial freedom is the result of a lifestyle obedient to the word of God.
11. It's always better to live smaller and more simply than to go into debt.

Taking It Home

- Look at the list of personal idols that you made last week. Select one item from the list and write ideas for how you can turn your focus away from that shiny god and toward the one true God.
- Referring back to Chapter 2 of *shiny gods*, write down the difference between the two kinds of debt: consumer debt and investment debt.
- Make a list of the bills that you must pay each month. Think about where your money is going. Do you need to make improvements in your financial transactions? If so, what will you do to change your financial habits?
- List ways you can simplify your lifestyle so that you live free of debt.

3. Be Faithful, Save, and Give

Planning the Session

Fundamentals
1. Confirm your meeting place and time.
2. Secure a TV and DVD player and ensure that they are operational.
3. Obtain extra copies of the book *shiny gods* to have on hand so that each participant will have a copy to use during the study session.
4. Have extra Bibles available for participants to use during the study session.
5. Secure paper and pencils for participants to use during a group activity.
6. Have available one or more paring knives, a large jar of peanut butter,* a bowl filled with birdseeds, plus paper plates, plastic knives, and an apple.
7. If your meeting area has Internet access, secure one or more computers and the necessary information for connecting to the Internet.

*If anyone in your group has allergies to nuts, substitute vegetable shortening for peanut butter.

Session Goals
This session is intended to help participants...
- understand that God wants to use us as channels through which his blessings and redemptive intentions flow to the world.
- realize that we can never anticipate future income; therefore, we need to live more simply so that we are ready for whatever the future holds.
- acknowledge that when we manage our money according to God's directives, our financial resources will grow.
- understand that generosity is God's design for wealth, and our generosity shows our thanksgiving to God.
- realize that faith is doing what God asks us to do, not complaining that we don't have the resources to accomplish his directives.

Key Insights
1. We are to be the channels through which God's blessings and redemptive intentions flow to the world.
2. God doesn't print money; God gives seed.
3. God's word tells us that we can never anticipate future income. Our intentional financial commitment today will provide for our family's financial well-being tomorrow.
4. Being righteous means rightly acting according to God's directives. When we are rightly acting according to God's directives with our money, we supply God's resources in the world.
5. Generosity is God's design for wealth, and our generosity shows our thanksgiving to God.
6. Faith is doing what God asks us to do, not complaining that we don't have the resources to accomplish his directives.

7. We need to live more simply so that we are ready for whatever the future holds.

Leader Background

- As we learn in this week's video segment, in 2005 Americans hit a negative savings rate for the first time when we began to spend a $1.22 for every dollar earned.
- During the economic downturn, Americans offset reduced income and unemployment by using credit or payday loans to cover their monthly expenses. This quick-fix solution threw Americans into increasingly deeper debt.
- Credit card debt is responsible for a major percentage of the total national debt. It is also a major cause of financial hardship for many Americans.
- In May 2011, total consumer debt in the U.S. reached $2.43 trillion.
- The average college student graduates with $20,000 of debt.
- Nearly one in five Americans aged 18-24 qualifies himself or herself as being in "debt hardship."
- Twenty-six percent of Americans admit to not paying their bills on time.
- Ginghamsburg Church's first Christmas Miracle Offering fed 26,000 people in 2005 via the agricultural program. It is now feeding 90,000 people.[10]

Getting Started

Opening Prayer

Heavenly God, thank you for the opportunity to gather in your name and study your word. Open our ears, our eyes, and our hearts to your will. Guide us to evaluate clearly and to apply to our own lifestyle the principles that we learn during this study. In Jesus' holy name we pray. Amen.

Biblical Foundation

He who supplies seed to the sower and bread for food will also supply and increase your store of seed and will enlarge the harvest of your righteousness. (2 Corinthians 9:10 TNIV)

Opening Activity

Have available one or more paring knives, a large jar of peanut butter, a bowl filled with birdseeds, paper plates, plastic knives, and an apple for each participant. Ask participants to cut their apples into sections, cover each apple section with peanut butter and then roll in the birdseeds.

Read 2 Corinthians 9:10, and point out that the treat they have made can provide food for several birds. Some will eat the seeds, some will eat the apple, and others will eat the seed and apple bits that fall to the ground. Point out that God provides for our needs, and he allows us extra so that we may share it with others, becoming a channel for God's blessings to flow to the world.

Learning Together

Video Presentation

Play Session 3: Be Faithful, Save, and Give
Running Time: 13:36

Group Discussion

We are to be the channels through which God's blessings and redemptive intentions flow to the world. John Wesley, founder of the Methodist movement, gave people three directives on the use of money. These directives are still relevant today. He said, "Earn all you can, save all you can, and give all you can."[11]

In 2 Corinthians 9:6-12, we read that God supplies seeds so that we may use them to enlarge his harvest. In other words, when he gives to us abundantly, we are to give to others abundantly. Our God-given resources are not meant to be hidden away. We are to use those resources to supply the needs of the Lord's people and to provide many expressions of thanks to God.

Mike Slaughter writes, "God doesn't print money; God gives seed." What do you think Slaughter means by this? What "seed" have you been aware of recently? Was that "seed" more valuable than printed money? How?

Point out that all of us have a responsibility to serve God's creation and to serve God's people through it. A number of studies over the past few years have demonstrated that people who give both time and finances are actually healthier than those who don't.[12] This phenomenon goes beyond age and economic status. Lead a discussion of the Acts 20:35 Scripture, "It's more blessed to give than to receive." Giving affects our openness to the Holy Spirit as well as our physical health.

Mike Slaughter writes that one reason for the success of Ginghamsburg Church's agricultural program in Darfur, Sudan, is that for every bag of seed they give to the farmer, the farmer has to return two bags after a successful harvest. One of those two bags is returned to the farmer to use for seed for the next growing season. The second bag is passed on to another family who will begin their own farm to support themselves. Discuss this concept and how it might apply in our own lives.

Ask participants if they have ever wondered why they are constantly struggling to make ends meet. Do they feel like they live paycheck to paycheck? Explain that when we hold on to our resources too tightly, we are preventing God from helping to make our resources grow. Read Mark 6:34-43.

Point out that had the disciples held onto the bread and fish, they would not have allowed Jesus to make the food grow and fulfill not just their own needs, but the needs of the crowd that had gathered to hear his teachings. Say, "Jesus doesn't accept our excuses; he knows what we have. We should not be focusing on our limitations, but turn our blessings over to God so that he can make them grow and fulfill his will."

Group Activity

If your meeting area has Internet access, go to http://www.youtube.com/watch?v=JRQE4Z136aY and allow the participants to view the YouTube video about the Sudan Project that Ginghamsburg Church supports. Point out that since January 2005, Ginghamsburg Church, along with its partner schools, churches and businesses has invested $4.4 million in sustainable humanitarian projects in Darfur, Sudan.[13]

If you do not have Internet access in your classroom, before the study go to http://www.thesudanproject.org and print some of the information to share with group participants.

Wrapping Up

Taking It Home

Remind the group that there are two resources available to help participants with personal application each week. First, there is the Participant Handout. Briefly review the Taking It Home exercises included on the handout. Encourage participants to complete the activities during the coming week.

Second, there is the book, *shiny gods*, which expands on the material covered in the weekly video presentations. Encourage participants to read the fourth chapter this week in preparation for next week's group session. Encourage participants who have not ordered or purchased copies of the book to do so now.

Notable Quote

Earthly goods are given to be used, not to be collected....
Hoarding is idolatry.[14]

—Dietrich Bonhoeffer

Closing Prayer

God, we want to follow your commands and obey you with all our heart. We pray that you will keep our path straight and our feet from stumbling. As we go through the coming week, help us to keep our focus on you and away from earthly desires. Amen.

3. Be Faithful, Save, and Give Participant Handout

You will be made rich in every way so that you can be generous on every occasion, and through us your generosity will result in thanksgiving to God. (2 Corinthians 9:11 TNIV)

Key Insights
1. We are to be the channels through which God's blessings and redemptive intentions flow to the world.
2. God doesn't print money; God gives seed.
3. God's word tells us that we can never anticipate future income. Our intentional financial commitment today will provide for our family's financial well-being tomorrow.
4. Being righteous means rightly acting according to God's directives. When we are rightly acting according to God's directives with our money, we supply God's resources in the world.
5. Generosity is God's design for wealth, and our generosity shows our thanksgiving to God.
6. Faith is doing what God asks us to do, not complaining that we don't have resources to accomplish his directives.
7. We need to live more simply so that we are ready for whatever the future holds.

Taking It Home
- Study your financial situation and make a sound, responsible fiscal plan of debt reduction, saving, and giving.
- What talents other than money has God entrusted to you that you can use to increase God's harvest? How can you begin using that talent to glorify God?

- Write out Proverbs 27:23-24. Then write what this verse means for you. Include how economic hard times may have affected you, your family, and your church. What actions did you take to offset the negative effects? What have you learned from that experience?

4. Heart Giving

Planning the Session

Fundamentals
1. Confirm your meeting place and time.
2. Secure a TV and DVD player and ensure that they are operational.
3. Obtain extra copies of the book *shiny gods* to have on hand so that each participant will have a copy to use during the study session.
4. Have extra Bibles available for participants to use during the study session.
5. Secure paper and pencils for participants to use during a group activity. Prepare handouts containing the words of Psalm 119:1-2.
6. Make or purchase an eight-inch layer cake for use in the group activity. Have additional cupcakes or cookies available for participants to eat after the activity if appropriate.

Session Goals
This session is intended to help participants...

- realize that we do not have to fear the economic consequences of the world; however, we must trust in God.
- recognize that what we do with what we have has the power to change the world.
- comprehend that as Christians, our wealth does not refer to money only; it refers to the seeds that God has placed in our hand—our talents, gifts, and resources—and we are accountable to God for using these resources to serve him.
- understand that no matter how big or small our field of influence, we are responsible for the well-being of all people regardless of their age, socioeconomic status, career choice, or anything else.
- understand that the reason people will believe us is not because we say the right words or believe the right things; they will believe us because they will see that we are committed to the right actions.

Key Insights

1. God has promised to provide for all our needs. He assures us that perfect love casts out all fear (1 John 4:18). Fear is not love; fear is not faith.
2. What we do with what we have has the power to change the world.
3. When the Bible refers to wealth, it's not talking about an abundance of money, but rather the seeds that God has placed in our hand—our talents, gifts, and resources
4. God has provided each of us with seeds for sowing and multiplying a crop of righteousness. We have accountability with God for using the resources that he has placed in our hands to serve God's redemptive purpose in the world.
5. One of the first and foremost purposes of wealth is to serve as God's means of provision in our own lives.
6. No matter how big or small our field of influence, we are responsible for the well-being of all people regardless of

their age, socioeconomic status, career choice, or anything else.

7. God names and claims the first ten percent of everything that enters our hands as the tithe.

8. God equips all of us to witness to the world through our generosity.

9. People will believe us not because we say the right words or believe the right things. They will believe us when they see that we are committed to right actions.

Leader Background

• Psalms found in the Bible are poetic expressions of the writer's feelings about God. They are shaped by the writer's fears, doubts, hardships, and joys. Some of the Psalms are written with a technique called parallelism—two lines of poetry that say the same thing in nearly the same way. For example, we read in Psalm 119:1-2 (GNT), "Happy are those whose lives are faultless, who live according to the law of the Lord. Happy are those who follow his commands, who obey him with all their heart."

• "Even the very poorest Americans—those at the second percentile of income in the United States—are at the sixty-second percentile globally."[15]

• The biblical tithe was part of the Mosaic Law. One-tenth of the produce of land and livestock would be given to support the Levitical priests.

• Seventy-seven percent of Americans say they were personally affected by the economic downturn of the early 2000s; twenty-eight percent say they were affected in a major way.

• During that economic downturn, twenty-eight percent of Americans reduced their giving to churches; twenty-four percent stopped giving to churches.[16]

Getting Started

Opening Prayer

Dear Lord, we praise your name. Bless this time of study and teach us your ways. Open our eyes, so that we may see the wonderful truths in your law. Accept our prayer of thanks, O Lord, and teach us your commands. Amen.

Biblical Foundation

"For where your treasure is, there your heart will be also." (Matthew 6:21)

Opening Activity

Provide paper and pencils or pens for each participant. Hand out the copies of Psalm 119:1-2 that you prepared ahead of time, and encourage those with Bibles to look up the entire psalm. Point out that psalms are poetic expressions of the writer's feelings about God. They can contain fears, doubts, hardships, and joys. Ask participants to write a prayer using Psalm 119 as a guide.

Learning Together

Video Presentation

Play Session 4: Heart Giving
Running Time: 8:45

Group Discussion

The word *wealth* as used in the Bible is usually not about an abundance of money. The biblical concept of wealth extends much further than mere silver or gold. It refers to the seeds that God has placed in our hand—our talents, gifts, and resources. Even in challenging economic times, what we do with these resources has the power to change the world.

Ask participants to refer to Chapter 4 of the book *shiny gods*. Ask, "When have you experienced heart giving? Were you the recipient or the giver?" Lead a discussion of sacrificial giving. Ask, "How can we give sacrificially during times of economic hardship?"

Leviticus 19:9 explains the law of sowing and reaping. No matter how big or small our "field," we are responsible for the well-being of all people regardless of their age, socioeconomic status, career choice, or anything else. We are not to pick our crop clean, but to leave some for "the poor and immigrants" to glean. Point out that the story of Ruth is a good example of gleaning the fields.

Refer the group of Mike Slaughter's cousin in this session's book chapter and video. Ask participants to describe the incident that changed her mind about Ginghamsburg Church. Lead a discussion of how our actions speak louder than our words.

God makes us rich in every way so that we may be generous in every way (2 Corinthians 9:11). From these riches that God so graciously gives us, he expects the first ten percent as a tithe. Even during difficult economic times, Christians are to provide for others and give a tithe to the Lord. Statistics show that during the recent economic downturn, many people cut back on giving; ministry and outreach programs received less money to operate; and missionaries received less support. "There is inadequate food in the Lord's house, because we are not trusting the Lord," says Mike Slaughter.

Ask participants to read about and discuss the sacrificial giving of the people at Ginghamsburg Church during their annual Christmas Miracle Offering.

Group Activity

Bring out the cake prepared earlier and place it on a table. Ask participants to gather while one participant cuts the cake. Tell the person cutting the cake to cut the whole cake making exactly ten pieces. Point out that it is difficult to get ten pieces from the small cake, and surely, a tenth of the cake would not be a lot to eat. However, God asks only one-tenth of what enters our hands, and he can spread it around the world.

Wrapping Up

Taking It Home

Remind the group that there are two resources available to help participants each week. First is the Participant Handout. Briefly review the Taking It Home application exercises included on the handout. Encourage participants to complete the activities during the coming week.

Second is the book *shiny gods*, which expands on the material covered in the weekly video presentations. If your group is planning a fifth week of study, encourage participants to read the conclusion this week in preparation for next week's group session. Encourage participants who have not ordered or purchased copies of the book to do so now.

Notable Quote

God nowhere tells us to give up things for the sake of giving them up. He tells us to give them up for the sake of the only thing worth having—viz., life with Himself. It is a question of loosening the bands that hinder the life.[17]

—Oswald Chambers

Closing Prayer

God, it is by your words that we can see where we are going. Throw a beam of light on our dark path as we go out into the world this week. Help us to see the opportunities that we have to tell others about your mercy and grace. In the name of your precious Son, amen.

4. Heart Giving
Participant Handout

*Those who are kind to the poor lend to the LORD, and he will
reward them for what they have done. (Proverbs 19:17 TNIV)*

Key Insights
1. God has promised to provide for all our needs. He assures
   us that perfect love casts out all fear (1 John 4:18). Fear is
   not love; fear is not faith.
2. What we do with what we have has the power to change
   the world.
3. When the Bible refers to wealth, it's not talking about an
   abundance of money. The Bible is talking about the seeds
   that God has placed in our hand—our talents, gifts, and
   resources
4. God has provided each of us with seeds for sowing and
   multiplying a crop of righteousness. We have accountability with God for using the resources that he has placed in
   our hands to serve God's redemptive purpose in the world.
5. One of the first and foremost purposes of wealth is to
   serve as God's means of provision in our own lives.
6. No matter how big or small our field of influence, we are
   responsible for the well-being of all people regardless of
   their age, socioeconomic status, career choice, or anything
   else.
7. God names and claims the first ten percent of everything
   that enters our hands as the tithe.
8. God equips us to witness to the world through our generosity.
9. People will believe us not because we say the right words
   or believe the right things. They will believe us when they
   see that we are committed to right actions.

Taking It Home

- Write your fears about the economic future for the nation, the church, yourself, and your family. Write out 1 John 4:18 underneath these fears you have listed. Pray about your fears, then turn them over to God, replacing your fears with faith.
- What seeds has God placed in your hands—your talents, gifts, resources? How are you using those seeds to serve God's redemptive purposes in the world? What can you do to witness to the world more generously?
- Examine your budget and decide to give a tithe to God.

Notes

1. Jim Forsyth, "Living Paycheck to Paycheck," *The Huffington Post,* September 20, 2012, http://www.huffingtonpost.com/2012/09/20/living-paycheck-to-paycheck_n_1899685.html.
2. Tommy Woodard and Eddie James, "Idol Worship," *SkitGuys.com,* February 1, 2010, http://www.youtube.com/watch?v=QPil9Br-5lE. Video is a promotion for the mini-movie *Idol Worship* by The Skit Guys.
3. Dwight L. Moody, *Secret Power or the Secret of Success in Christian Life and Work* (New York: Fleming H. Revell, 1881), The Project Gutenberg EBook, http://www.gutenberg.org/files/33341/33341-h/33341-h.htm#c2.
4. Ben Woolsey and Matt Schulz, "Credit Card Statistics, Industry Facts, Debt Statistics," *CreditCards.com*, http://www.creditcards.com/credit-card-news/credit-card-industry-facts-personal-debt-statistics-1276.php
5. "Consumer Debt Statistics," *Consolidated Credit Counseling Services, Inc.,* http://www.consolidatedcredit.org/credit-card-debt/consumer-debt-facts/#back.
6. The five statistics above from Woolsey and Schulz, *CreditCards.com.*
7. Matthew DeCarlo, "Americans Spent Over $15 Billion on Video Games in 2010," *TechSpot,* http://www.techspot.com/news/41991-americans-spent-over-15-billion-on-video-games-in-2010.html.
8. Douglas McIntyre, Michael Sauter, and Charles Stockdale, "Ten Things Americans Waste the Most Money On," 24/7 Wall St., February 24, 2011, http://247wallst.com/2011/02/24/ten-things-americans-waste-the-most-money-on/#ixzz2MDxe7Wac http://247wallst.com/2011/02/24/ten-things-americans-waste-the-most-money-on/#ixzz2EDHHWPUj.
9. Mike Slaughter, *shiny gods* (Nashville: Abingdon Press, 2013), 60.
10. "The Sudan Project," *Ginghamsburg.org,* http://ginghamsburg.org/serve/places_to_serve/the_sudan.
11. John Wesley, "The Use of Money," Sermon 50, *Works* 2: 266–80.
12. Christine S. Moyer, "Volunteering Can Boost Physical and Mental Health," *American Medical News,* January 17, 2012, http://www.ama-assn.org/amednews/2012/01/16/hlsb0117.htm.
13. Ginghamsburg Church, "Sudan Project Overview 2010," *GinghamsburgChurch,* December 22, 2010, http://www.youtube.com/watch?v=JRQE4Z136aY.

14. Dietrich Bonhoeffer, *The Cost of Discipleship* (New York: Touchstone, 1995), 175.

15. Suzy Khimm, "Does America's 99 Percent Represent the Top 1 Percent on Earth?", *The Washington Post,* October 12, 2011, http://www.washingtonpost.com/blogs/ezra-klein/post/does-americas-99-percent-represent-the-top-1-percent-on-earth/2011/10/12/gIQA5JVQfL_blog.html.

16. This and the previous statistic are from Barna Group, "Donors Proceed with Caution, Tithing Declines," *Barna Group,* May 10, 2011, http://www.barna.org/donorscause-articles/486-donors-proceed-with-caution-tithing-declines.

17. Oswald Chambers, *My Utmost for His Highest,* (Ulrichsville, OH: Barbour, 2000), 6.

CPSIA information can be obtained at www.ICGtesting.com
Printed in the USA
LVOW100708210313

325048LV00002B/5/P